GEOFACTS

POPULATION
AND
SETTLEMENT
GEO FACTS

Izzi Howell

Crabtree Publishing Company
www.crabtreebooks.com

Crabtree Publishing Company

www.crabtreebooks.com
1-800-387-7650

Published in Canada
Crabtree Publishing
616 Welland Avenue
St. Catharines, ON
L2M 5V6

Published in the United States
Crabtree Publishing
PMB 59051
350 Fifth Ave, 59th Floor
New York, NY 10118

Published in 2018 by CRABTREE PUBLISHING COMPANY.

First published in 2017 by The Watts Publishing Group
Copyright © The Watts Publishing Group 2017

Author: Izzi Howell

Editors: Izzi Howell, Ellen Rodger

Design: Rocket Design (East Anglia) Ltd

Editorial director: Kathy Middleton

Proofreader: Angela Kaelberer

Prepress technician: Abigail Smith

Print and production coordinator: Margaret Amy Salter

Photographs

Alamy: Trinity Mirror/Mirrorpix 18, Lou Linwei 29b; iStock: Niko Guido 6, ferrantraite 25, scottnz 28; Shutterstock: Donatas Dabravolskas 7t, Valeriya Anufriyeva 8t, mTaira 8b, Prometheus72 10t, zaferkizilkaya 10b, De Visu 11, Karve 12, Brothers Good 14, 15r and 26, imtmphoto 15l, Patrick Poendl 16, NEstudio 17t, jbor 17b, Maxisport 19, jagoda 20–21, S-F 21t, Nadezhda1906 22t, Sentavio22b, 197188484 23l, Sorin Colac 23r, donsimon 27tl, shadow216 27tr, saiko3p 27b, Tumar 29t; Techtype: 7b, 13 and 16–17.

All design elements from Shutterstock: Kazmin Aleksei, Blablo101, Macrovector, ksaverius, Faber14, Meilun, ProStockStudio, Seita, Alexzel, NotionPic, ivector, Sevenpixels, Rimma Zaynagova, lady-luck, user friendly, Jenniki, mOleks.

Printed in the USA/122019/BG20171102

Library and Archives Canada Cataloguing in Publication

Howell, Izzi, author
          Population and settlement geo facts / Izzi Howell.

(Geo facts)
Includes index.
Issued in print and electronic formats.
ISBN 978-0-7787-4385-9 (hardcover).--
ISBN 978-0-7787-4407-8 (softcover).--
ISBN 978-1-4271-2018-2 (HTML)

          1. Population--Juvenile literature. 2. Human geography--Juvenile literature. 3. Human settlements--Juvenile literature. I. Title.

HB883.H69 2018   j304.6   C2017-906907-1
                                        C2017-906908-X

Library of Congress Cataloging-in Publication Data

CIP available at the Library of Congress

Contents

What are Population and Settlement?

Humans live all over the world and have settled permanently on every continent except Antarctica. **Settlements** where people can live together, such as villages, towns, and cities, can be found across the globe.

USA (page 13)

Population

We use the word population to describe the number of people living in an area. This can be a city, a country, a continent, or even the world. The world population is currently 7.4 billion and growing every day. Experts think that it will reach 10 billion by 2056.

! If everyone on Earth today stood shoulder-to-shoulder, they would fill an area the size of Los Angeles, California—around 501 square miles (1,300 sq km).

FOCUS ON Uganda (page 14)

Settlements

A settlement is a place where people live. Settlements can be tiny, such as single houses in **rural** areas, or huge, such as massive cities. Most settlements are located near resources such as drinking water, building materials, and **fertile** land.

FOCUS ON UK (page 18)

Read on to find out about population and settlements in these areas.

FOCUS ON Japan (page 15)

FOCUS ON Athens (page 22)

FOCUS ON Manila (page 26)

India (page 13)

Distribution and Density

The population of the world is unevenly **distributed**. Overall, there are more empty areas than crowded areas. In almost every country, there are areas where people live close together and areas where they live far apart.

Distribution

Some continents and countries have a high population. Asia is the continent with the highest population, with over 4.4 billion people, while only 0.39 billion people live in Oceania. In general, more people live in lower-income and middle-income countries than in higher-income countries.

China
1.38
billion

Africa
1.21
billion

More people live in the country of China than on the continent of Africa.

Lower-income, or poorer, countries can find it hard to recover from natural disasters. In Haiti, some people are still homeless after the devastating earthquake in 2010.

Countries and income

We can categorize countries by the average amount of money that each resident earns. Most of the time, people in lower- and middle-income countries have lower **life expectancies**, less education, and a lower standard of living than people in higher-income countries. Many people in lower-income countries work in jobs where they create or process raw materials. However, there are also people who live in poverty in higher-income countries.

Countries such as Brazil are difficult to categorize as middle or high income. Brazil has a growing economy and many trade deals, but there are still people who live in great poverty.

Developing a population

Lower- and middle-income countries tend to have higher populations, as they have higher **birth rates**. This is because people have little access to **family planning** and need to have a large number of children who will work to provide money for the family. Lack of health care in these countries also means that children are less likely to live to adulthood. Having multiple children increases the chance of some surviving to adulthood.

! Most areas of high density are in the Northern Hemisphere.

Density

Population **density** is the number of people living in an area, usually a square mile (km). Small countries, such as Monaco, usually have the highest population densities. Within countries, the highest levels of density are in cities and along the coasts, where it is difficult for settlements to expand.

The Equator

Sparsely populated

Moderately populated

Densely populated

Population Growth

The world population has grown massively in the past hundred years. The number of births and deaths every year affect how the world population grows.

History

For most of human history, the world population has been very low—around several tens of millions. People couldn't grow enough food to support a high population, and life expectancies were short. By 1000 C.E., the population had reached 400 million, but it didn't reach 1 billion until 1804.

Births and deaths

If there are more births than deaths in an area, the population will increase. More deaths than births will result in a decrease. Health care is also important. In the past 200 years, more children have reached adulthood due to improvements in health care and **sanitation** and have been able to reproduce, which boosted the birth rate.

The world population shot up in the 1900s, growing from 2 billion in 1927 to over 7 billion today. However, the rate of growth has slowed down now, so the world population will increase more slowly in the near future.

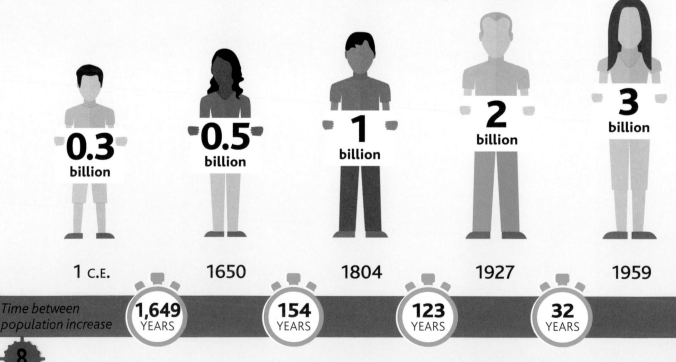

	0.3 billion	0.5 billion	1 billion	2 billion	3 billion
	1 C.E.	1650	1804	1927	1959
Time between population increase	1,649 YEARS	154 YEARS	123 YEARS	32 YEARS	

Around the world

There is a large difference in population growth between countries with different incomes. As lower- and middle-income countries have very high birth rates and high **death rates**, their population is growing. Higher-income countries have low birth and death rates, which means that their population is staying the same. Some countries, such as Ukraine, have such low birth rates that their population is decreasing.

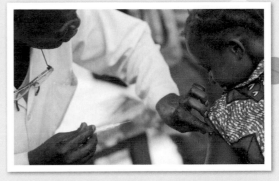

*This girl in the Democratic Republic of Congo is about to be vaccinated against tetanus. Vaccines have helped to improve **life expectancy** rates.*

Japan's population decreased by 204,000 people in 2011, 16,000 of whom lost their lives in the March 2011 tsunami.

Population change

Population is affected by factors such as large-scale **epidemics**, wars, and natural disasters. **Immigration**, or people coming into a country, and **emigration**, or people leaving a country, also have an impact on a country's population.

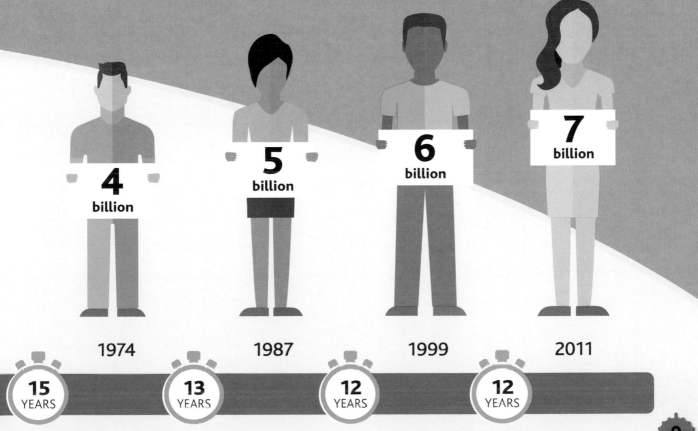

4
billion

5
billion

6
billion

7
billion

1974   1987   1999   2011

15 YEARS   **13** YEARS   **12** YEARS   **12** YEARS

FOCUS ON Overpopulation

With the world population at its highest point ever and still growing, experts often wonder how many people Earth can actually support. Some people question if the lack of resources and space in some areas is a result of **overpopulation**.

Water

Large populations need a lot of water, which is hard to get as our climate becomes hotter and drier. Many places around the world, such as the Middle East and California, have experienced serious **droughts** and do not have enough water to support their population.

*Drought also affects farms, as farmers do not have enough water to **irrigate** their crops. This means crops die, and there is less food available.*

Resources

A high population puts pressure on resources such as coal, oil, gas, and certain metals. Supplies of these resources are running low and may even run out entirely. Our modern lifestyle also uses more resources than ever before. For example, in the past, coal was only used for cooking and heating, but now it is also burned in large amounts to create electricity.

Food

One in nine people around the world do not have enough food to live a healthy life. The problem isn't that enough food can't be produced. Modern farming techniques allow farmers to grow large amounts of crops. In fact, some countries even throw excess food away. The issue is supply, as most food grown in low-income countries is exported for a **profit**, rather than sold at a fair price to people who live there.

Overfishing is affecting fish populations around the world. If we do not fish sustainably and let populations recover, many species of fish may become extinct.

In 2013, around 102.5 million tons (93 metric tons) of fish were caught worldwide.

Garbage

We are creating more waste than ever before. Much waste, such as plastics, won't break down for thousands of years. Waste is dumped into the sea or left in landfill sites, which take up valuable space that could be used for housing or **agriculture**.

Space

Although Earth is mainly empty of people, some areas are incredibly overcrowded. These tend to be cities and **urban** areas that can't expand for geographical reasons, such as a coastline, or for environmental reasons, such as protected nearby countryside. Many overcrowded areas suffer housing shortages, with people living in terrible, cramped conditions.

In Ho Chi Minh City, Vietnam, there is not enough affordable housing to go around. Some people are forced to live in shanties, while the rich live in new apartment blocks.

1 person in North America uses 198 pounds (90 kg) of resources a day.

1 person in India uses 22 pounds (10 kg) of resources a day.

Solutions

The key to solving the problem of overpopulation may not be reducing the number of people, but instead changing how we use resources and space. Most resources are used by a small number of people who live in high-income countries. Often, people in these countries are wasteful. If these countries used fewer resources, there would be more than enough to go around. For example, in cities, space-efficient apartments could be built rather than giant luxury mansions.

Gender and Age

The population of an area is made up of people of different **genders** and ages. It's important to have a balanced population so that people can reproduce and care for the young and the old.

Around the world

Higher-income countries usually have low birth rates and high life expectancies, which results in more old people than young people. Low- and middle-income countries experience the opposite effect. In theory, all countries should have an equal number of men and women. However, this can be affected by war or prejudices.

Average across the world
1.03 boys
for every girl

In China
1.15 boys
for every girl

Population pyramids

We can show the structure of a population using a diagram called a **population pyramid**. Population pyramids look different in every country.

LARGE OLDER POPULATION
From 1946 to 1964, there was a great increase in the birth rate called the **baby boom**. Those born at that time are now in their 50s, 60s, and 70s. "Boomers" are shifting the population balance.

POPULATION GROWTH
From 1975 to 2010, India's population doubled in size. This is because of better nutrition and immunization from diseases. India is expected to have the world's highest population by 2030.

! Between 1979 and 2015, to control its booming population, China had a policy that allowed families to have only one child. Many preferred that child to be a boy. Many girls were adopted in other countries. Because of this, by 2020, there could be 35 million more men than women in China.

VERY HIGH BIRTH RATE
The average woman in India has 2.48 children. This high birth rate is expected to continue in the future.

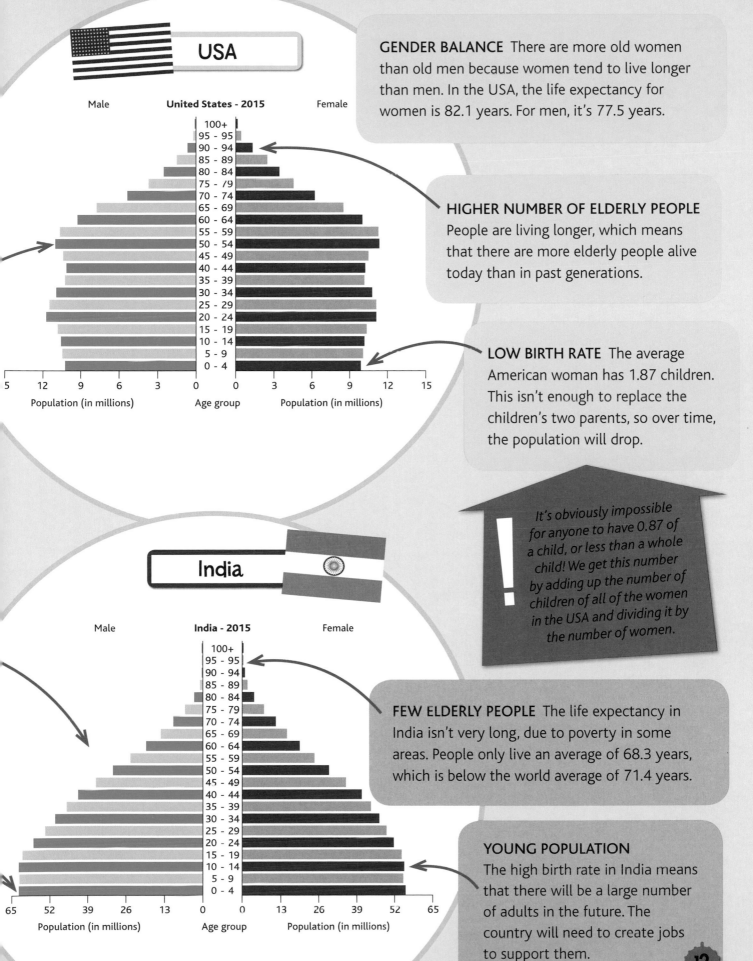

USA

Male   **United States - 2015**   Female

Age groups: 100+, 95 - 95, 90 - 94, 85 - 89, 80 - 84, 75 - 79, 70 - 74, 65 - 69, 60 - 64, 55 - 59, 50 - 54, 45 - 49, 40 - 44, 35 - 39, 30 - 34, 25 - 29, 20 - 24, 15 - 19, 10 - 14, 5 - 9, 0 - 4

Population (in millions): 15, 12, 9, 6, 3, 0 | 0, 3, 6, 9, 12, 15

Population (in millions)   Age group   Population (in millions)

GENDER BALANCE There are more old women than old men because women tend to live longer than men. In the USA, the life expectancy for women is 82.1 years. For men, it's 77.5 years.

HIGHER NUMBER OF ELDERLY PEOPLE People are living longer, which means that there are more elderly people alive today than in past generations.

LOW BIRTH RATE The average American woman has 1.87 children. This isn't enough to replace the children's two parents, so over time, the population will drop.

! It's obviously impossible for anyone to have 0.87 of a child, or less than a whole child! We get this number by adding up the number of children of all of the women in the USA and dividing it by the number of women.

India

Male   **India - 2015**   Female

Population (in millions): 65, 52, 39, 26, 13, 0 | 0, 13, 26, 39, 52, 65

Population (in millions)   Age group   Population (in millions)

FEW ELDERLY PEOPLE The life expectancy in India isn't very long, due to poverty in some areas. People only live an average of 68.3 years, which is below the world average of 71.4 years.

YOUNG POPULATION The high birth rate in India means that there will be a large number of adults in the future. The country will need to create jobs to support them.

13

Uganda and Japan

The countries of Uganda and Japan are very different. Their population sizes, geographic location, cultures, economies, and governments contribute to these differences. Where people live is a major factor in determining how well and how long they live.

Uganda

Uganda is a small, landlocked country in east Africa with a population of 37 million people. It is one of the poorest countries in the world.

Standard of living

20 percent of Ugandans live in poverty and don't make enough money to buy food. As most of the land is used for commercial farming, people can't grow enough of their own food. In the recent past, diseases such as **HIV/AIDS** killed many people. Today, new drugs and disease prevention have helped many Ugandans live healthier and longer.

FACT

★ 2% of the population is 65 or over, as many adults died from HIV/AIDS related illnesses.
★ 50% of the population is between 0–14 years
★ life expectancy is 54.93 years

Population change

Uganda has a high birth rate, as few people have access to family planning. Some families rely on their children to contribute to the household income. About 25 percent of children in Uganda work. The population is growing so fast that the country may have a serious problem with overpopulation in the future.

FACT

★ 5.89 children per woman
★ population has grown by over 10 million people in the last 10 years

Distribution

Agriculture is one of the biggest industries in Uganda. Many people live in rural areas, where jobs can be found. Rural areas have less access to clean drinking water and sanitation, which increases the chances of disease.

FACT

★ 84% live in rural areas

Japan

The country of Japan is spread over several islands in the north Pacific Ocean. It has a population of 127 million people. Japan is a great world power with a huge **economy** and high standard of living.

Standard of living

Japan has a low poverty rate and a good health care system, with plenty of doctors and hospitals. The Japanese diet, which traditionally contains a lot of fish and rice, is considered one of the healthiest in the world.

FACT
★ 25% of the population is over 65 years old
★ life expectancy is 84.74 years

Population change

Japan's population is decreasing due to falling birth rates. Many people are choosing not to have children. In the future, there may not be enough people to support the country's industries or look after the older generation. Japan is considering encouraging immigration or giving extra money to people who have more children.

Distribution

As Japan is made up of islands, there is a limited amount of space to use for housing. People tend to live in cities, which is where most of the jobs are. In cities, people live in apartments. Families are often small, so there is no need for large homes.

FACT
★ 93.5% live in cities

FACT
★ 1.4 children per woman
★ population growth is -0.16%, so the population is getting smaller over time

Migration

People have always moved around. The first humans moved constantly, looking for food and shelter. Today, people often move to cities or countries for economic, social, political, or environmental reasons.

Push factors

The reasons why **migrants** leave an area are known as push factors because they "push" people into going. Some leave through choice, and others are forced to go.

- Unemployment or joblessness
- Poor services, such as health care and education
- Crime
- War
- Environmental disaster, such as earthquakes
- Persecution, or mistreatment because of religion, politics, or sexuality

Some important current migration routes

The border between Mexico and the USA is heavily protected to stop people crossing over without the correct paperwork.

Moving around

Most countries don't allow people to freely enter whenever they want. Immigrants usually need to have a document that gives them the right to live and work in a country, such as a **visa**. Some people immigrate illegally, which makes it difficult for them to find jobs and access health care. Some countries, such as Australia, encourage some types of immigration and will give visas to skilled people.

It is easier for immigrants to Russia to become citizens if they speak Russian. Russia has recently made its immigration laws simpler, as they hope that immigration will help to remedy its decreasing population.

Pull factors

Migrants choose to come to an area for many reasons. These are known as pull factors.

- Jobs
- Services provided by the country such as health care
- Safety from war or conflict
- Climate
- Better standard of living
- To be near family

Many South Asian men have found construction work in Dubai, helping to build the new structures that are springing up across the city.

FOCUS ON

🇬🇧 UK Migration

The United Kingdom (UK) is a desirable destination for immigration and receives thousands of immigrants every year. However, many UK citizens also choose to emigrate to other countries.

History

There have been several waves of immigration to the UK throughout history. In the 1800s, many people from Ireland traveled to the UK. After the Second World War, the UK received immigrants from former British **colonies**, such as India and Jamaica. Recently, people from other parts of Europe have come to the UK for better work and pay.

🇺🇸 USA

the Caribbean

By the 1970s, many schools across the UK had pupils from a range of different backgrounds.

Emigration

In the 1800s, over 11 million people emigrated from the UK. Some left through choice. Some were found guilty of crimes and were sent away as punishment to Australia and the USA. Today, people continue to leave the UK, looking for jobs, a better standard of living, and warmer weather. Around 5.5 million UK citizens currently live overseas.

Refugees

Every year, the UK receives **refugees**, or people who have fled their home country because of war or danger due to their beliefs or ethnic background. Like many countries, the UK believes it has a responsibility to help refugees and offer them protection. Some refugees are allowed to stay in the UK permanently.

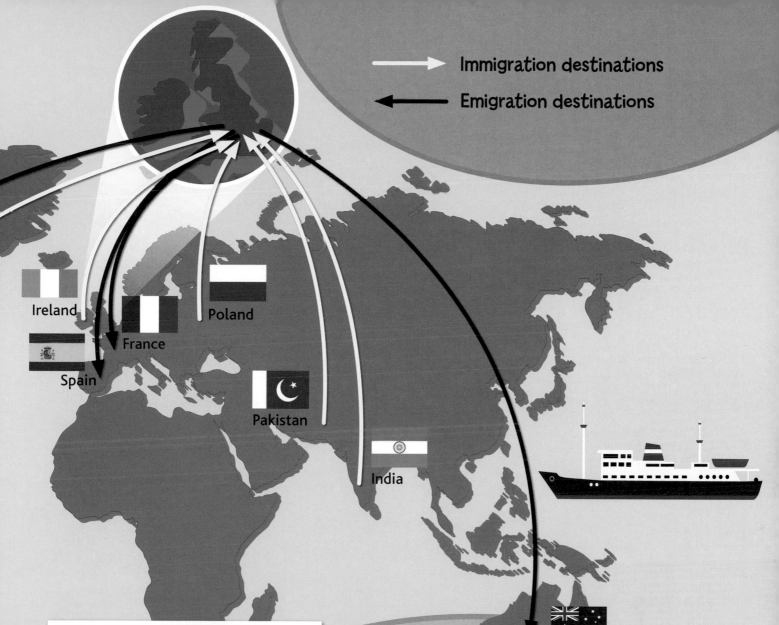

Immigration destinations

Emigration destinations

Ireland

France

Spain

Poland

Pakistan

India

Australia

Impact

Migration has a positive and a negative impact on the country left behind and the country where migrants settle. Some positive effects of immigration include more people to work and pay taxes. Immigrants bring their culture, foods, and beliefs to their adopted country and make it more diverse. They also embrace the culture, sports, and ideas of their new homes.

Many immigrants make huge contributions to society. Mo Farah was born in Somalia, but is now a British citizen who lives and trains in the USA. He is one of the most successful modern track athletes and also runs a charity.

Settlement Sites

Many modern towns and cities stand on the sites of ancient settlements. The locations of ancient settlements were carefully chosen for reasons that benefited past civilizations and which are still helpful for the current residents.

Early settlements

The first humans were hunter-gatherers, moving around in search of food and shelter. Around 12,000 years ago, people started farming and had to settle permanently in order to tend to their crops. This led to the construction of the first small villages.

Growing towns

Farming allowed people to grow enough food to support a larger population. As the population grew, so did the towns and villages. Successful settlements were built in areas that had a good supply of drinking water, or fertile land for growing crops.

Resources

In the past, it was very difficult for people to transport building supplies, such as stone and wood, so it was important for settlements to be close to forests and quarries. Modern settlements also benefit from being close to resources, as they provide jobs for residents.

Landscape

Flat land was easier to build on, as most early civilizations did not have the technology to build on hillsides. Today, architects design buildings that can stand on steep slopes.

Water supply

As well as access to clean drinking water, the residents of early settlements needed fresh water to irrigate their crops. Modern cities can filter and clean dirty water or remove the salt from seawater to make it drinkable.

Safety

The best settlement sites were far from dangers such as floods, volcanoes, and earthquakes. However, it was hard for people to anticipate risks as many years passed between natural disasters. Today, we have developed ways to predict and protect ourselves from natural disasters, but they can still be very destructive.

Defense

Although it was easier for early civilizations to build on flat land, high towers and castles were much easier to defend. Not only could they see enemies coming, but it also gave them an advantage in battle, as it is much harder to fight uphill.

The ruins of Pompeii in Italy show the dangers of building a settlement close to a volcano. The town was never rebuilt after its destruction from erupting Mount Vesuvius in 79 C.E.

Transport links

Settlements often developed along trade routes, which went across land and sea. A steady stream of traders passing through brought money and goods to the settlement. River settlements also provided transportation to visitors, with boats to carry passengers across rivers.

Fertile land

All civilizations need access to fertile land in which crops can grow well. Early settlements needed to grow enough food to support their population. It would have been too expensive and difficult to bring in food from elsewhere. With more food, a settlement could feed a larger population.

Athens

Athens is the capital city of Greece. It is found in the southeast part of the country. The site has been inhabited since at least 5,000 B.C.E. and has been home to several civilizations.

The long history of Athens can be seen in the mixture of old and new buildings found in modern Athens. The old buildings attract many tourists.

History

The best-known people to live in Athens were the ancient Greeks. Athens has also been occupied by many empires, including the Roman Empire, the Byzantine Empire, and the Ottoman Empire. Today, Athens is an important global city and trade center.

The Acropolis

The high flat rock in the center of Athens is known as the Acropolis. The first settlers of Athens probably started their settlement on the Acropolis as it is easy to defend and gives a great view of the surrounding plain. Later, the ancient Greeks built temples on the Acropolis, many of which still stand today.

Landscape

Athens is built on a mainly flat plain, which is surrounded by four mountains. This was a good landscape for an ancient settlement, but it does create an unfortunate weather condition for a modern city. The mountains trap warm air high up, which stops ground pollution and fog from escaping up into the atmosphere. As a result, Athens suffers from high levels of pollution.

Resources

Rocks such as marble and limestone can be found in the mountains that surround Athens. This local marble has been used for many buildings in Athens throughout history. In ancient Athens, people also gathered wood from the trees that grow on the mountainsides.

Sea

Athens is located around 12 miles (20 km) from the sea, on an inlet that is easy to defend. This location helped with trade in Athens. Boats could easily bring and take goods from the city. Today, the port of Piraeus is one of the busiest passenger ports in Europe, bringing millions of tourists to Athens every year.

marble

This is an aerial view of Athens, with the Acropolis and the coastline clearly visible.

The ancient Greeks built the Erechtheion temple from marble taken from nearby Mount Pentelikon.

Food

Although the climate around Athens is generally dry, some fertile farming land can be found along nearby rivers. The sea supplies the city with large amounts of fish and shellfish. In the past, the wealth of Athens from trade also allowed the city to import food.

Settlement Layout

The layout of a settlement depends on the landscape of the area where it is built. However, we can see some similarities in the layout of most settlements.

Center

Settlements usually grow outward, so the center is often the oldest area. Government and administration buildings are found in the city center, along with businesses and offices.

Housing

In the inner and outer city, there is mostly housing with a few businesses to support residents. Inner-city housing is often older than outer-city housing. This contributes to some of it being more run-down. In the suburbs, people live in carefully planned communities with newer housing and facilities such as recreation centers.

Density

Density is usually high in the center of a city. It decreases as you move out of the city toward the suburbs. In the inner city, people often live in apartments, which is the least wasteful way of housing many people in a small space. In the suburbs, people tend to live in houses with large yards.

suburbs

outer city

inner city

central business area

The city center and business district of Los Angeles is relatively small compared to the massive urban sprawl of housing and small businesses.

Limits

When cities grow bigger, they spread out into the surrounding countryside. This is known as **urban sprawl**. Sometimes they reach and join up with other nearby settlements. Some cities, such as London, are surrounded by a **greenbelt** to stop the city expanding further.

linear settlement

Countryside

Rural settlements also have their own shapes. They can be linear (line-shaped), nuclear (gathered around one point) or scattered, with houses in no particular pattern. Villages are often nuclear, based around a religious building or community center.

nuclear settlement

scattered settlement

FOCUS ON Manila

Manila is the capital city of the Philippines, a country in southeast Asia made up of thousands of islands. Manila is a bustling, crowded city with the highest population density in the world.

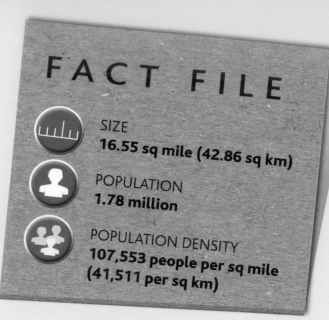
Landscape

Manila is located on the coast, which means that the sea limits how far it can expand. The growth of Manila is also restricted by swampland to the north of the city and mountains to the west. These make it difficult to build on.

Economy

There are many important government offices in Manila. It is the capital city of the Philippines. There is also a large business and finance district in the center, as Manila is an important business center in the Pacific region. Its port brings cargo and tourists to the city.

Manila

People

Most residents of Manila are Filipino, but there are small communities of Chinese and American immigrants. Many Filipinos have left the countryside to find work in cities such as Manila.

26

It is very difficult to find cheap housing in Manila. Poor people live in makeshift homes called barong-barong. Barong-barong are made from scrap metal and wood and have no running water, electricity, or sewers.

Many historic buildings in Manila were destroyed during World War II. They were replaced with new buildings that housed a higher density of people. However, there is still a serious housing shortage in Manila, as people are not able to build enough housing to keep up with the growing population.

New apartments in Manila are often built far away from businesses where people work. People spend many hours commuting to work.

There are many types of vehicles on Manila's congested streets, including jeepneys. These are small buses made from old military jeeps.

Transport

Manila was not designed for a large amount of traffic. The many cars create terrible traffic jams. The traffic also leads to high levels of air pollution. There are plans to build elevated roads, which should improve conditions on the ground.

Changing Settlements

Settlements must adapt over time to suit the needs of their changing population. It's important to rebuild and upgrade settlements as they get older, while preserving their history and culture in neighborhoods and buildings.

Growing population

People move to cities for many reasons. Some migrate from rural areas for school and jobs. Others immigrate from other countries and settle in cities. As the population grows, cities must grow too. Today, people want to live in larger homes than in the past, meaning more land is used for housing.

In 60 years, the size of an average newly built house in the USA has more than doubled.

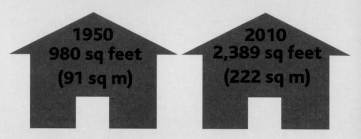

1950
980 sq feet
(91 sq m)

2010
2,389 sq feet
(222 sq m)

Regeneration

Some cities demolish old, run-down buildings in inner city areas and industrial sites that are no longer used, such as docks and factories. The land is used for new housing or offices. However, some cities improve and adapt abandoned buildings to keep the character of the neighborhood.

Melbourne Docklands in Melbourne, Australia, used to be unused warehouses and dock buildings. The old buildings have been torn down and replaced with modern offices, shops, and apartments.

Gentrification

Rebuilding areas usually makes life better for local residents. However, this improvement can make the area so desirable to live in that house prices and rent in the neighborhood go up, which makes it too pricey for lower-income residents. The process of fixing up lower-income neighborhoods for middle- and upper-income people is known as gentrification. Many cities that have undergone gentrification, such as San Francisco, are now only affordable for the very rich.

The residents of this artists' community in Berlin moved in because of the cheap rents. Now, the neighborhood is being gentrified, and people want to tear down the artists' community and build new luxury apartment buildings.

New cities

Some countries with a lot of available space can build new settlements from scratch. However, it's important to make sure that there is a demand for a new city or town and enough jobs to encourage new residents. Some countries such as Spain have ghost towns, or large finished settlements that are totally empty. The lack of good jobs means people can't afford to live there.

The city of Kangbashi was built in northern China in 2003. It contains enough homes for around 300,000 people, but only around 100,000 actually live there.

29

Glossary

agriculture Growing crops and looking after animals that will be used for food

baby boom A large increase in the number of babies born during a particular time

birth rate The number of babies born in a period of time

colonies Countries or territories settled and ruled by another country or empire

death rate The number of people who die over a period of time

density The number of people living in a specific area, usually a square mile (or km)

distributed How something is spread across an area

drought A long period when there is not enough rain and people do not have enough water

economy The system by which a country produces and uses goods and money

emigration When people leave a country or an area for another

epidemic When lots of people get the same disease at the same time

family planning Controlling how many children you have

fertile Describes land where plants can grow well

greenbelt A strip of countryside around a city where building is not allowed

HIV/AIDS A serious disease that affects the immune system and causes death if left untreated

immigration People coming to a country or an area

irrigate To bring water to an area of land

life expectancy The amount of time that a person is expected to live

migrants People who leave an area or country to find a new permanent residence

overpopulation A situation in which there are too many people for the amount of resources and space available

population pyramid A diagram that shows the population structure in an area

profit Money that you get for selling goods at a higher price than they cost to produce

refugee Someone who is forced to leave their home because of war or threats to their safety

rural Relating to the countryside

sanitation A way of protecting people's health by removing waste and dirt

settlement A place where humans have settled and live permanently, such as a town

urban Relating to a city

urban sprawl The spread of a city into the area surrounding it

visa A document that you need to enter or work in a country where you are not a citizen

Test yourself!

1. Which continent has the highest population?

2. In which year did the world population reach one billion?

3. Which country encouraged people to only have one child?

4. Why is Japan's population decreasing?

5. Name two push factors that encourage people to migrate.

6. Which part of a settlement is usually the oldest?

7. What is a nuclear settlement?

8. Which country is Manila the capital of?

Check your answers on page 32.

Further reading

Mapographica: Your World in Infographics
Jon Richards, Ed Simkins (Crabtree, 2017)

Investigating Human Migration and Settlement
Paul Challen, Marina Cohen, Sally Morgan, Ceri Oeppen, Natalie Hyde, Robert Walker (Crabtree, 2010)

Websites

Read more about population and settlement at the following websites:

www.3dgeography.co.uk/settlement-geography

www.worldometers.info/world-population/

www.sciencekids.co.nz/sciencefacts/topten/countriesbypopulation.html

Index

Answers

1 Asia (over 4.4 billion people)

2 1804

3 China

4 Because of falling birth rates.

5 Some push factors include crime, war, unemployment, environmental disasters, and persecution.

6 The center

7 A settlement gathered around one point.

8 The Philippines